WATERMELON

Life Cycles

ABDO
Publishing Company

A Buddy Book
by **Julie Murray**

VISIT US AT
www.abdopublishing.com

Published by ABDO Publishing Company, 4940 Viking Drive, Edina, Minnesota 55435.

Copyright © 2007 by Abdo Consulting Group, Inc. International copyrights reserved in all countries. No part of this book may be reproduced in any form without written permission from the publisher. Buddy Books™ is a trademark and logo of ABDO Publishing Company.

Printed in the United States.

Coordinating Series Editor: Sarah Tieck
Contributing Editor: Michael P. Goecke
Graphic Design: Deb Coldiron
Cover Photograph: Photos.com
Interior Photographs/Illustrations: Fotosearch, Media Bakery, National Watermelon Promotion Board (watermelon.org), Photos.com

Library of Congress Cataloging-in-Publication Data

Murray, Julie, 1969–
    Watermelon / Julie Murray.
        p. cm. — (Life Cycles)
    Includes index.
    ISBN-13: 978-1-59928-712-6
    ISBN-10: 1-59928-712-9
    1. Watermelons—Life Cycles—Juvenile literature. I. Title.

SB379.W38M87 2007
635'.615—dc22

2006031420

Table Of Contents

What Is A Life Cycle?

Watermelons are living things. The world is made up of many kinds of life. People are alive. So are toucans, dolphins, giraffes, and grasses.

Los sandias son cosas vivas. El Mundo esta echo con muchos tipos de vida. Los humanos estan vivos. Tambien los tucanes, delfines, jirafas, y el pasto.

A watermelon undergoes many processes before you can slice it and take a bite.

una sandia necesita muchos Presesos antes de comerla

Every living thing has a life cycle. A life cycle is made up of many changes and **processes**. During a life cycle, living things are born, they grow, and they **reproduce**. And eventually, they die. Different living things start life and grow up in **unique** ways.

What do you know about the life cycle of the watermelon?

All About Watermelon

Watermelon is a fruit that grows on a vine. There are more than 1,200 different kinds of watermelons. Each melon has a **unique** taste and **texture**. Each kind also looks different.

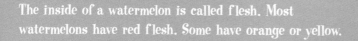

The inside of a watermelon is called flesh. Most watermelons have red flesh. Some have orange or yellow.

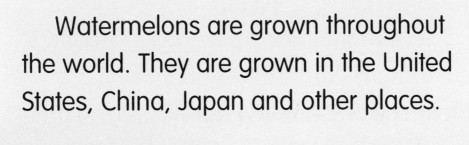

Watermelons are grown throughout the world. They are grown in the United States, China, Japan and other places.

Watermelons can be enjoyed in several ways. Many people eat freshly cut watermelon fruit. Others dry watermelon seeds to eat. Watermelons are used in other ways, too. Factories make them into products such as juice.

Cold watermelon juice is tasty!

Watermelon can be cut into pieces and eaten.

9

A Watermelon's Life

A watermelon begins life as a seed. Watermelon grows best in places with mild and warm weather.

A watermelon blossom.

A watermelon's growing cycle starts in spring. At this time, green vines begin to grow. Eventually, flowers bud on the vines.

Throughout the summer months, the blooms turn into watermelon fruit. The fruit grows bigger and bigger. When the watermelon is fully grown, it is time to pick it. Then, you can eat it! Have you ever picked a watermelon to eat?

Guess What?

…Watermelons are made up of more than 90 percent water.

…Early explorers used watermelons to store and carry drinking water.

Watermelons are grown on every continent except Antarctica.

…China grows the most watermelons in the world. The United States is the fourth-leading producer of watermelon.

…Watermelon is native to Africa. In fact, the first watermelon was picked in Egypt about 5,000 years ago. Early Egyptians even drew pictures of watermelon on walls!

In some parts of the world, people buy cube-shaped watermelons. They are grown this way to fit more easily in refrigerators.

Starting To Grow

Watermelon fruit grows on a vine. Each watermelon has a green rind on the outside and fleshy fruit on the inside. This flesh is usually red. It can also be orange or yellow.

Most watermelons have black seeds and white seeds. But some watermelons do not have any seeds.

Watermelon plants start from watermelon seeds.

Though watermelons start small, they can grow to be very large. Watermelons can weigh as little as two to four pounds (one to two kg). Or, they can be as big as 44 pounds (20 kg) or more!

Watermelon plants start from the seeds inside a watermelon. Once planted, the seeds sprout in the ground and become tiny watermelon plants.

Sun and rain help the plants grow into long vines. Watermelon vines can grow more than six feet (two m) in one month!

From Seed To Melon

Watermelon vines are called runners. Runners can reach lengths of 40 feet (12 m) or more. In the warm months, these vines produce yellow flowers.

Insects such as bumblebees help **pollinate** the watermelon blossoms. When this happens, the watermelon vines begin to grow fruit.

Each vine may produce 2 to 15 watermelons.

After about 60 days, tiny watermelon fruits appear on the vines. Over the warm summer months, these watermelon fruits grow bigger and bigger.

Ready To Eat

It takes 75 to 100 days after planting for watermelons to fully develop and **ripen**. When the watermelons are ripe, it is time to harvest them.

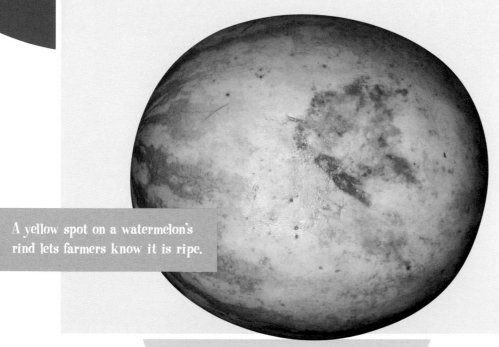

A yellow spot on a watermelon's rind lets farmers know it is ripe.

Trucks take watermelons to grocery stores. There, people buy them and take them home to enjoy the juicy fruit.

A watermelon's rind looks hard. But, watermelons break easily. So, workers must pick them by hand.

Once the watermelons have been harvested, workers prepare them to be sold. Today, grocery stores sell both whole and sliced watermelons. And, seedless watermelons are quite popular.

Endings And Beginnings

After its fruit is harvested, the watermelon vine dies. Death is the end of one watermelon plant's life. But, it is not the end of all watermelons.

Most watermelons have seeds and can **reproduce**. So, their **species** continues on.

When a vine produces new watermelon fruits, it helps create a new **generation** of watermelons. This is the beginning of another life cycle.

Watermelon is a healthy snack. It contains vitamins that your body needs.

Can You Guess?

Q: What parts of a watermelon can people eat?
A: All of them! You can eat the seeds, the rind, and the flesh.

Q: When did the word "watermelon" first appear in an English dictionary?
A: In 1615.

People can eat every part of a watermelon fruit.

Important Words

generation a group that is living at the same time and is about the same age.

pollinate transferring pollen from the flower of one plant to another plant. This helps the plant grow fruits and seeds.

process a way of doing something.

reproduce to produce offspring, or children.

ripe fully developed and matured. Ready to be eaten.

species living things that are very much alike.

texture the way something feels when touched.

unique different.

Web Sites

To learn more about watermelon, visit ABDO Publishing Company on the World Wide Web. Web site links about watermelon are featured on our Book Links page. These links are routinely monitored and updated to provide the most current information available.

www.abdopublishing.com

Index